CONNECT BIBLE STUDIES

How t[illegible]od

Nick Hornby

(Viking, 2001)

Marriage
Being Good
Being Bad
Guilt

www.connectbiblestudies.com
connect
linking the Word to the world

CONNECT BIBLE STUDIES: How to be Good

Published in this format by Scripture Union, 207-209 Queensway, Bletchley, MK2 2EB, England.

Scripture Union is an international Christian charity working with churches in more than 130 countries providing resources to bring the good news about Jesus Christ to children, young people and families — and to encourage them to develop spiritually through the Bible and prayer.

As well as a network of volunteers, staff and associates who run holidays, church-based events and school Christian groups, Scripture Union produces a wide range of publications and supports those who use the resources through training programmes.

Email: info@scriptureunion.org.uk
Internet: www.scriptureunion.org.uk

Damaris Trust enables people to relate Christian faith and contemporary culture. It helps them to think about the issues within society from a Christian perspective and to explore God's truth as it is revealed in the Bible. Damaris provides resources via the Internet, workshops, publications and products.

Email: office@damaris.org
Internet: www.damaris.org

ALSO AVAILABLE AS AN ELECTRONIC DOWNLOAD: www.connectbiblestudies.com

Chief editor: Nick Pollard
Consultant Editor: Andrew Clark
Managing Editor: Di Archer
Written by Di Archer, Caroline Puntis, Tony Watkins

First published 2001
ISBN 1 85999 610 8

British Library Cataloguing-in-Publication Data: a catalogue record for this book is available from the British Library.

Cover design and print production by:
CPO, Garcia Estate, Canterbury Road, Worthing, West Sussex BN13 1BW.

Other titles in this series:

Harry Potter and the Goblet of Fire ISBN 1 85999 578 0
The Matrix ISBN 1 85999 579 9
U2: All that you can't leave behind ISBN 1 85999 580 2
Billy Elliot ISBN 1 85999 581 0
Chocolat ISBN 1 85999 608 6
Game Shows ISBN 1 85999 609 4
Destiny's Child: Survivor ISBN 1 85999 613 2

And more titles following — check www.connectbiblestudies.com for latest titles or ask at any good Christian bookshop.

www.connectbiblestudies.com

connect

linking the Word to the world

Using Connect Bible Studies

What Are These Studies?

These innovative home group Bible studies have two aims. Firstly, we design them to enable group members to dig into their Bibles and get to know them better. Secondly, we aim to help members to think through topical issues in a Biblical way. Hence the studies are based on a current popular book or film etc. The issues raised by these are the subjects for the Bible studies.

We do not envisage that all members will always be able to watch the films or read the books, or indeed that they will always want to. A summary is always provided. However, our vision is that knowing about these films and books empowers Christians to engage with friends and colleagues about them. Addressing issues from a Biblical perspective gives Christians confidence that they know what they think, and can bring a distinctive angle to bear in conversations.

The studies are produced in sets of four — i.e. four weeks' worth of group Bible Study material. These are available in print published by Scripture Union from your local Christian bookshop, or via the Internet at www.connectbiblestudies.com. Anyone can sign up for a free monthly email newsletter that announces the new studies and provides other information (sign up on the Connect Bible Studies website at www.connectbiblestudies.com/uk/register).

How Do I Use Them?

We design the studies to stimulate creative thought and discussion within a Biblical context. Each section therefore has a range of questions or options from which you as leader may choose in order to tailor the study to your group's needs and desires. Different approaches may appeal at different times, so the studies aim to supply lots of choice. Whilst adhering to the main aim of corporate Bible study, some types of questions may enable this for your group better than others — so take your pick.

Group members should be supplied with the appropriate sheet that they can fill in, each one also showing the relevant summary.

Leader's notes contain:

1. Opening Questions

These help your group settle in to discussion, whilst introducing the topics. They may be straightforward, personal or creative, but are aiming to provoke a response.

2. Summary

We suggest the summary of the book or film will follow now, read aloud if necessary. There may well be reactions that group members want to express even before getting on to the week's issue.

3. Key Issue

Again, either read from the leader's notes, or summarised.

4. Bible Study

Lots of choice here. Choose as appropriate to suit your group — get digging into the Bible. Background reading and texts for further help and study are suggested, but please use the material provided to inspire your group to explore their Bibles as much as possible. A concordance might be a handy standby for looking things up. A commentary could be useful too, such as the New Bible Commentary 21st century edition (IVP, 1994). The idea is to help people to engage with the truth of God's word, wrestling with it if necessary but making it their own.

Don't plan to work through every question here. Within each section the two questions explore roughly the same ground but from different angles or in different ways. Our advice is to take one question from each section. The questions are open-ended so each ought to yield good discussion — though of course any discussion in a Bible study may need prompting to go a little further.

5. Implications

Here the aim is to tie together the perspectives gained through Bible study and the impact of the book or film. The implications may be personal, a change in worldview, or new ideas for relating to non-churchgoers. Choose questions that adapt to the flow of the discussion.

6. Prayer

Leave time for it! We suggest a time of open prayer, or praying in pairs if the group would prefer. Encourage your members to focus on issues from your study that had a particular impact on them. Try different approaches to prayer — light a candle, say a prayer each, write prayers down, play quiet worship music — aim to facilitate everyone to relate to God.

7. Background Reading

You will find links to some background reading on the Connect Bible Studies website:
www.connectbiblestudies.com/

8. Online Discussion

You can discuss the studies online with others on the Connect Bible Studies website at
www.connectbiblestudies.com/discuss/

www.connectbiblestudies.com

connect

linking the Word to the world

How to be Good

Nick Hornby (Viking, 2001)

Part One: Marriage

You see, I don't want a divorce. OK, I know I did, before, when I didn't know what it meant and I didn't know what I felt and I didn't know how awful the prospect would seem — but now I don't, and I'm (almost) positive I'd do (almost) anything to get my marriage back on track.

(Katie, p. 50)

Please read Using Connect Bible Studies *before leading a Bible study using this material.*

Opening Questions

Choose one of these questions.

How did you react to *How To Be Good?*	Is marriage still valid in the twenty-first century?
Describe a married couple you admire and say why.	As a group, list ten characteristics of a good marriage.

Summary

Katie can no longer remember the exact moment when things started to turn sour in her marriage to David, but it is clear that there has been a progressive deterioration in communication. She now tells their story with apathetic bitterness: 'The row isn't worth talking about, really: it's just a row, between two people who actually don't like each other enough not to row,' (p. 21).

David's cynical demeanour has taken its toll on Katie, who resorts to a brief affair in order to feel some human warmth. This leads her to question whether she wants to stay married to David and when the opportunity arises, she asks him for a divorce. David does not want a divorce until he finds out about Katie's affair. However, following a dramatic change of heart, he realises that he must take his share of the blame: 'I haven't loved you enough, and I'm really sorry. I do love you, and I haven't communicated that properly or positively'

(p. 54). Although he wants to stay married now, David's conversion brings new problems so Katie moves into a bedsit. Here is the solitude she has been yearning for — she has time to read a book, listen to CDs and simply be Katie, rather than Katie the doctor, wife or mother. What she cannot escape is the need to make a decision about her marriage. In the end, she decides to go home and carry on, but is uncertain that her future will ever bring the satisfaction she longs for.

Key Issue: Marriage

The plot of *How To Be Good* revolves around the relationship struggles between Katie and her husband, making marriage a big issue in this book. With the different crises they face, and the lifestyle changes they make, their marriage is under pressure. Katie and David bicker their way through the opening chapters showing all the telltale signs of a marriage suffering stress. This conflict — and Katie's affair — seem typical of today's society. So our studies begin with marriage as a key issue. Is marriage just a semi-useful human convention, or is there a biblical foundation for it? What does it mean to be committed to a long-term relationship? How should marital conflicts be handled? And how do we deal with conflict in other close relationships? At the end of the book, Katie thinks she has found an answer in her need for refreshment and renewal — recharging her batteries seems to help to get life and marriage back on track. Does this really work, and what is a biblical way to maintain a marriage?

Bible Study

Choose one question from each section.

1. Ignition — getting married

... getting married — or finding a partner whom we will want to spend our lives with and have children by — is on our agenda. It's something we know we will do one day, and if you take that away from us then we are left with promotions at work and the possibility of a winning lottery ticket, and it's not enough ... (Katie, p. 86)

Leaders: You may like to bear in mind Ephesians 5:31, 32 as you discuss these questions — it may add an extra dimension to your thinking.

- Read Genesis 2:18–25. Why did God make woman? What is marriage for? What is the reason referred to in verse 24?

- Read Matthew 19:3–12. Why does Jesus take marriage so seriously? Is marriage for everyone?

  Leaders: The focus here should be on marriage rather than divorce. Obviously, this is a big issue for many people, however, so we have included some useful links on the background reading page on the Connect Bible Studies website (see below).

2. Long distance — commitment

This is not the life I chose for myself. Except that is not true, either, because I did choose, I suppose, when I said that I would marry David for richer, for poorer, in sickness and in health, as long as we both shall live ... What did I think I was choosing, when I married David? What do any of us think we are choosing? If I try to recapture now the semi-formed fantasies I had then, I'd say that they erred on the side of prosperity and health. (Katie, p. 84)

- Read Malachi 2:13–16. Why is God not moved by the people's tears (v.13)? Why does it matter so much to God when we break faith with one another?

  Leaders: After the exile, the people of Judah became apathetic about the law of Moses. Intermarriage with unbelievers — and the subsequent divorces — became a major problem.

- Read Hosea 2:1–3:5. How does God demonstrate commitment to his people in the face of their unfaithfulness to him? How does God feel about them?

  Leaders: God asked Hosea to marry an adulterous wife in order to demonstrate God's attitude to his unfaithful people. Hosea's naming of his children, his rejection of his wife and finally his reconciliation with her were all prophetic actions.

3. Traffic jam — conflict

It shouldn't be like this. This isn't the way it's supposed to be. If it had been what we thought and what we did, there wouldn't be anything to argue about, because we had thought and done it together, but the only thing we have managed to do together is create an enormous mess ... (Katie, p. 41)

- Read Ecclesiastes 7:1–22. How does the writer bring a sense of perspective to conflict? Which verses would help to deal with conflict in marriage?

- Read Ephesians 4:22–5:2. Why are these verses particularly relevant to the marriage relationship? What do they say about how we handle conflict?

4. Recharging batteries — marriage maintenance

'Katie, in the last couple of months you've had an affair and you moved out of our house. You're not exactly a blushing bride, are you? The point is, what are we going to do when we're both so, so ... soul-dead? Me, I feel like I've come too far down one road to go back. And maybe you feel like that about our marriage. And that means that whatever we do is going to be really, really hard, much harder than it would be for anyone else who knew what they wanted and why. We've both got flat batteries, but we've still got to drive the car somehow. And I haven't got a clue how to do that. Have you?'
(David, p. 225)

- Read Psalm 23. How does our relationship with God restore us? How can this help a marriage relationship?

- Read Ephesians 5:25–33. How does Paul say a husband and wife should care for each other and themselves? Why?

Implications

'I'm not looking for forgiveness. I want to talk about it. I want to explain. I want you and I to go out and attempt to communicate. As husband and wife.' (Katie, p. 206)

Choose one or more of the following questions. We recognise that the subject matter is potentially delicate – it might be worth thinking through how you would handle group members who are genuinely struggling with relationship conflict, or who have messed things up in the past.

- How important is communication in marriage? What difference does God make?
- How do you handle conflict in marriage or close relationships? Are there attitude changes you could make in the light of today's study?
- How do we stick at long-term commitment, in marriage or elsewhere, in a world which favours get-out clauses?
- What can we do to guard ourselves — and others — from having an affair?
- If you are married, what precautions do you take to avoid burning out? In general, how does God recharge your batteries?
- Are there apologies you need to make? Is there forgiveness you need to offer?

Prayer

Spend some time praying through these issues.

Background Reading

You will find links to some background reading on the Connect Bible Studies website: www.connectbiblestudies.com/uk/catalogue/0007/background.htm

Discuss

Discuss this study in the online discussion forums at www.connectbiblestudies.com/discuss

Members' Sheet: How to be Good — Part 1

Summary

Katie can no longer remember the exact moment when things started to turn sour in her marriage to David, but it is clear that there has been a progressive deterioration in communication. She now tells their story with apathetic bitterness: 'The row isn't worth talking about, really: it's just a row, between two people who actually don't like each other enough not to row,' (p. 21).

David's cynical demeanour has taken its toll on Katie, who resorts to a brief affair in order to feel some human warmth. This leads her to question whether she wants to stay married to David and when the opportunity arises, she asks him for a divorce. David does not want a divorce until he finds out about Katie's affair. However, following a dramatic change of heart, he realises that he must take his share of the blame: 'I haven't loved you enough, and I'm really sorry. I do love you, and I haven't communicated that properly or positively' (p. 54). Although he wants to stay married now, David's conversion brings new problems so Katie moves into a bedsit. Here is the solitude she has been yearning for — she has time to read a book, listen to CDs and simply be Katie, rather than Katie the doctor, wife or mother. What she cannot escape is the need to make a decision about her marriage. In the end, she decides to go home and carry on, but is uncertain that her future will ever bring the satisfaction she longs for.

Key Issue

Bible Study notes

Implications

Prayer

www.connectbiblestudies.com

connect

linking the Word to the world

How to be Good

Nick Hornby (Viking, 2001)

Part Two: Being Good

I'm a good person. In most ways. But I'm beginning to think that being a good person in most ways doesn't count for anything very much, if you're a bad person in one way. Because most people are good people, aren't they?

(Katie, p. 48)

Please read Using Connect Bible Studies *before leading a Bible study using this material.*

Opening Questions

Choose one of these questions.

Does doing the 'right' thing make you feel better? Why?	Why do you think people give to charities?
Why do people want to be good?	Why do you think Katie's children assumed that going to church was part of being good?

Summary

Until recently, Katie had never been in any doubt about what it means to be good: 'Listen: I'm not a bad person. I'm a doctor. One of the reasons I wanted to become a doctor was because I thought it would be a good — as in Good, rather than exciting or well-paid or glamorous — thing to do' (p. 6). When her angry and irritating husband, David, goes to see the mysterious healer, DJ GoodNews, for a physical ailment but returns having had all traces of cynicism removed from his character, Katie's world is thrown into turmoil. David is determined to make the world a better place — he immediately sets about solving the homelessness problem and starts to write a book called *How to be Good.* As far as Katie is concerned, all David's good deeds just make her look bad.

Meanwhile, their marriage is struggling to survive and the children, Tom and Molly, are trying to adapt to the new regime. Molly sides with David and goes along with all his moral crusades; Tom and Katie are united in resisting David's inarguable logic as he gives away their possessions and Sunday lunch. Somehow, Katie's efforts never seem to be good enough. She knows that she hasn't been a perfect wife and mother, but she has at least made every effort to be a good doctor, even battling to support her quota of incurable 'heartsink' patients. In the end, she feels that if she can just keep the family going, that will be good enough.

Key Issue: Being Good

So what does it mean to be good? The title of Nick Hornby's book gives away its central theme. Suddenly released from his anger and cynicism, David just wants to be good. Katie has always wanted to help people but is thrown into confusion by her husband's new approach. In our studies, we pick out three major themes that *How to be Good* explores. Does being good mean being religious and going to church? Does it mean taking up the cause of the homeless and living your life for social action? Or does being good mean doing the 'right' thing morally? What does the Bible say about being good? Is it really an action, or is it something different?

Bible Study

Choose one question from each section.

1. Looking good — doing the religious thing

I have just invited one of my heartsink patients around to eat with us once every couple of weeks for ever. A few months ago this would have been a surefire indication of my own barminess, and yet now it signifies only a cold-hearted and pragmatic sanity. I feel like getting out of the car and dancing on the roof. Molly will take the news much harder than Brian, but that's the thing with this brand of charity. It's all about what it does for us, not for people like Brian. (Katie, p. 233)

- Read Isaiah 1:10–20. God had asked for sacrifices from his people (see for example Leviticus 1), so why did he now object to them? What did he really want?

- Read Matthew 15:1–20. Why wasn't Jesus satisfied with the Pharisees' religiousness? What did Jesus see as the real issue?

  Leaders: The traditions of the Pharisees said that a son could avoid his responsibility to his parents by declaring the money that might have gone to them as korban *— a gift devoted to God, set aside for the temple treasury.*

2. Doing Good — doing the social action thing

The word 'charity' reels me back in. '"Charity vaunteth not itself, is not puffed up",' the man with the puff says. Hurrah for St Paul! Right on! Vaunting and puffing! Puffing and vaunting! You want any of that, you should come round to Webster Road, which has become a Puffers and Vaunters Social Club! Why had I never heard this stuff properly before? (Katie, p. 189)

- Read Matthew 6:1–4. Why, according to Jesus, do some people do good things in public? What does Jesus recommend instead?

- Read 1 Corinthians 13. What might someone be hoping to gain through the actions described in verses 1–3? Why don't they count without love? What do you think is the significance of 1 Corinthians 13 for Kate in *How to be Good?*

3. Feeling good — doing the moral thing

I am seriously beginning to worry about Molly's mental health: how many eight-year-olds would want to spend day after day doing something so unappealing just to show that they are morally superior to a sibling? (Katie, p. 182)

- Read Luke 7:36–50. What did Simon think of the woman? Compare their attitudes towards Jesus. How did Jesus' story challenge Simon?

- Read Luke 15:11–32. Why did the older brother feel that he had been treated unfairly? Where did he go wrong?

4. Made good — being transformed

It's not enough to be a doctor, you have to be a good doctor, you have to be nice to people, you have to be conscientious and dedicated and wise, and though I enter the surgery each morning with the determination to be exactly those things, it only takes a couple of my favourite patients — a Barmy Brian, say, or one of the sixty-a-day smokers who are aggressive about my failure to deal with their chest complaints — and I'm ill-tempered, sarcastic, bored. (Katie, p. 179)

- Read 2 Peter 1:1–11. How does Peter say we should be good? What is the balance between what God does and what we do?

- Read Romans 3:9–31. What does Paul say about our attempts to be good? How does God make us good? What responsibilities does this leave us with?

Implications

Who are these people, that they want to save the world and yet they are incapable of forming proper relationships with anybody? As GoodNews so eloquently puts it, it's love this and love that, but of course it's so easy to love someone you don't know, whether it's George Clooney or Monkey. Staying civil to someone with whom you've ever shared Christmas turkey — now there's a miracle. (Katie, p. 220)

Choose one or more of the following questions.

- Be honest — do you sometimes put on a 'Christian' mask when you are actually unhappy inside about your relationship with God? How can you be more real, and help others to be the same?
- How do you feel about social action? Are you motivated to change your world? Why?
- Does doing the right thing with the wrong motive cancel it out? What is God looking for in our attitudes towards morality?
- What would you say to the Katie and David about their attempts to be good?
- Why doesn't going to church make you good? What would you say to a friend who thinks they are not good enough to go to church?
- Do you think your church services would help a newcomer to experience the presence and love of God? If not, what needs to be changed?

Prayer

Spend some time praying through these issues.

Background Reading

You will find links to some background reading on the Connect Bible Studies website: www.connectbiblestudies.com/uk/catalogue/0007/background.htm

Discuss

Discuss this study in the online discussion forums at www.connectbiblestudies.com/discuss

Members' Sheet: How to be Good — Part 2

connect

Summary

Until recently, Katie had never been in any doubt about what it means to be good: 'Listen: I'm not a bad person. I'm a doctor. One of the reasons I wanted to become a doctor was because I thought it would be a good — as in Good, rather than exciting or well-paid or glamorous — thing to do' (p. 6). When her angry and irritating husband, David, goes to see the mysterious healer, DJ GoodNews, for a physical ailment but returns having had all traces of cynicism removed from his character, Katie's world is thrown into turmoil. David is determined to make the world a better place — he immediately sets about solving the homelessness problem and starts to write a book called *How to be Good.* As far as Katie is concerned, all David's good deeds just make her look bad.

Meanwhile, their marriage is struggling to survive and the children, Tom and Molly, are trying to adapt to the new regime. Molly sides with David and goes along with all his moral crusades; Tom and Katie are united in resisting David's inarguable logic as he gives away their possessions and Sunday lunch. Somehow, Katie's efforts never seem to be good enough. She knows that she hasn't been a perfect wife and mother, but she has at least made every effort to be a good doctor, even battling to support her quota of incurable 'heartsink' patients. In the end, she feels that if she can just keep the family going, that will be good enough.

Key Issue

Bible Study notes

Implications

Prayer

www.connectbiblestudies.com

connect

linking the Word to the world

How to be Good

Nick Hornby (Viking, 2001)

Part Three: Being Bad

I couldn't work out who was right and who was wrong, my house was full of people I didn't know ... I was going mad, really. So I had to do this, didn't I? And of course it's selfish and indulgent and bad, but it seemed at the time as though I couldn't work out how to be good without being bad.

(Katie, p. 167)

Please read Using Connect Bible Studies *before leading a Bible study using this material.*

Opening Questions

Choose one of these questions.

In the book, do you think Katie ended up 'being bad'?	How do you feel if you have done something wrong?
How would you define 'being bad'?	Do you think some people want to 'be bad'? Why?

Summary

'David, you make your living from being aggrieved,' says Katie to her husband David, who writes a column — 'The Angriest Man in Holloway' — for the local paper. His entire life revolves around criticising others' opinions, beliefs and courses of action. Over the years, David's anger and cynicism have seeped into every corner of his life, including his marriage. Katie has had enough of the permanent scowl and resorts to being bad herself — she has an affair and asks David for a divorce.

Then a strange thing happens. David undergoes a kind of spiritual conversion and starts being good. He begins by giving away his children's possessions, which infuriates the rest of the family. His daughter Molly soon takes David side — largely in order to spite her brother, Tom, who finds the transition particularly difficult and starts stealing at school. Katie now has to struggle with new definitions of what being bad and being good really mean. For example, was owning all those material possessions really bad? Yet she cannot help being angry at what she sees as David's over-the-top attempts to be good and at his relationship with his guru, DJ GoodNews. Now she has become cynical instead of David. After GoodNews moves in, Katie begins to find life in the family home intolerable and moves out — although she keeps this a secret from the children. Having always been the moral conscience of the family, Katie now finds herself relegated to the moral low-ground against David's smug goodness.

Key Issue: Being Bad

In Hornby's book, David attempts to be good partly by jettisoning from his life all that he considers to be bad. So out go cynicism and anger, two of his erstwhile trademarks. 'The Angriest Man in Holloway' now wants to erase all that spurious anger from his life. Out too go several material possessions, along with the drive to obtain them. He and GoodNews even attempt to make up for past crimes against others, only to discover that not being bad is harder than they thought. What could be gained by ridding themselves of anger, cynicism and possessions? Does the Bible say these things are indeed bad? What of their attempts to make amends — why did 'being human' mean that these failed?

Bible Study

Choose one question from each section.

1. 'Only I'm any good' — anger

And here I am ... outraged that my son and daughter aren't allowed to keep what is theirs, and yet still, somehow on the wrong side, an agent of the forces of darkness ... I don't know what to say. The frightened, unhappy children of frightened, unhappy women have nothing; we have two of everything. We give away some, a tiny fraction, of what we have too much of. What is there for me to be angry about?
(Katie, p. 73)

- Read Genesis 4:1–16. Why did Cain get angry? Where did his anger lead him? What was God's perspective on the whole situation?

  Leaders: It is not immediately clear why Cain's offering was less pleasing to God than Abel's — note that Cain merely brought 'some' of the fruits whereas Abel brought 'fat portions from some of the firstborn of his flock', i.e., a better sacrifice. See also Hebrews 4:11.

- Read Jonah 3 and 4. Did Jonah have any right to be angry? How did God try to change Jonah's perspective?

2. 'Only things are any good' — materialism

Can I be a good person and spend that much money on overpriced consumer goods? I don't know. But I do know this: I'd be no good without them. (Katie, p. 243)

- Read Deuteronomy 8:1–20. In what way can material security tempt us away from God? How can we develop a right attitude to possessions?

- Read Mark 10:17–31. What did the rich young man lack? Why is it hard for a rich person to enter the kingdom of God?

  Leaders: Jewish culture believed that wealth was a sign of God's favour.

3. 'Nothing's any good' — cynicism

I had become comfortable with his cynicism, and in any case, we're all cynical now, although it's only this evening that I recognise this properly. Cynicism is our shared common language, the Esperanto that actually caught on, and though I'm not fluent in it ... I know enough to get by. (Katie, p. 131)

- Read Nehemiah 4:1–6. What did Sanballat hope to achieve with his cynical taunts? How did the Jews respond?

- Read Ecclesiastes 1:1–11. Why does the writer of Ecclesiastes see everything as meaningless? What emotions does his cynicism lead to?

4. 'Can we be any good?' — being human

David: ***'[GoodNews] shouldn't have said that. I'm very disappointed in him. We're supposed to be above all that.'***
Katie: ***'But we're not, are we?'***
David: ***'I'm not talking about you. I'm talking about me and him.'***
Katie: ***'That's the trouble, isn't it? You were human all the time. You just forgot.'***
(p. 219)

- Read Psalm 51. What does David think about his state of sinfulness? What hope does he have for his condition?

- Read Romans 7:7–8:4. What does Paul say about whether we can be good? How does he explain the way out of our dilemma?

Implications

I almost find myself feeling sorry for David — it's sad, after all, that what certainly appears to be a genuine attempt to convey warmth and concern should be met with such naked mistrust — but ten years of ill-temper are not easily forgotten, and David has been grumpy for as long as Tom has been alive. (Katie, p. 62)

Choose one or more of the following questions.

- Why do we tend to think of ourselves as right and everyone else as wrong? What effect does this have on others?
- Do you have a problem with anger — your own or others'? How can you let God in on this?
- Examine your attitude towards material security and possessions. How can you trust God more?
- If you are prone to cynicism, do you know why? Does it hold you back from trusting and adventuring with God?
- Why do you think communities become cynical? How as Christians can we combat this, either in society or in people we meet?
- How would you answer a friend who says: 'I'm not a bad person really, I've never murdered or stolen — I don't need God'?

Prayer

Spend some time praying through these issues.

Background Reading

You will find links to some background reading on the Connect Bible Studies website: www.connectbiblestudies.com/uk/catalogue/0007/background.htm

Discuss

Discuss this study in the online discussion forums at www.connectbiblestudies.com/discuss

Members' Sheet: How to be Good — Part 3

Summary

'David, you make your living from being aggrieved,' says Katie to her husband David, who writes a column — 'The Angriest Man in Holloway' — for the local paper. His entire life revolves around criticising others' opinions, beliefs and courses of action. Over the years, David's anger and cynicism have seeped into every corner of his life, including his marriage. Katie has had enough of the permanent scowl and resorts to being bad herself — she has an affair and asks David for a divorce.

Then a strange thing happens. David undergoes a kind of spiritual conversion and starts being good. He begins by giving away his children's possessions, which infuriates the rest of the family. His daughter Molly soon takes David side — largely in order to spite her brother, Tom, who finds the transition particularly difficult and starts stealing at school. Katie now has to struggle with new definitions of what being bad and being good really mean. For example, was owning all those material possessions really bad? Yet she cannot help being angry at what she sees as David's over-the-top attempts to be good and at his relationship with his guru, DJ GoodNews. Now she has become cynical instead of David. After GoodNews moves in, Katie begins to find life in the family home intolerable and moves out — although she keeps this a secret from the children. Having always been the moral conscience of the family, Katie now finds herself relegated to the moral low-ground against David's smug goodness.

Key Issue

Bible Study notes

Implications

Prayer

www.connectbiblestudies.com

connect

linking the Word to the world

How to be Good

Nick Hornby (Viking, 2001)

Part Four: Guilt

David knows I feel guilty about just about everything ... I end up making a mental list of the things I feel guilty about, and whether there is anything I can do about making any of it better. What alarms me just how easy it is to remember things I've done wrong, as if they are floating on the surface of my consciousness all the time and I can simply skim them off with a spoon. I'm a doctor, I'm a good person, and yet there's all this stuff ...

(Katie, p. 178)

Please read Using Connect Bible Studies *before leading a Bible study using this material.*

Opening Questions

Choose one of these questions.

Is there anything you feel guilty about that you really shouldn't?	What do your friends tend to feel guilty about?
Do you think everyone feels guilty sometimes?	Why is feeling guilty so uncomfortable?

Summary

As a GP, Katie has always found plenty to feel guilty about — she constantly has to deal with patients who are let down through lack of resources and drugs that never work. Recently, though, her guilty conscience has thrived on personal troubles that she certainly has more control over. Problems with her husband, David, have affected the whole family. Katie feels particularly guilty now that she has secretly moved out of the family home to live in a bedsit: 'I have woken most nights since then at 2.25 am precisely, feeling bereft and lonely and guilty and frantic with worry and fear, and it takes me ages to get back to sleep. And yet I wake up in the morning feeling fresh,' (p. 172). Herein lies the source of her anxiety — she feels that it is her duty to be at home but she wants and needs the space to get her life back together.

Katie recognises the deep-rooted need to be forgiven and start over again, but cannot see a realistic way that this can be achieved. Instead, she reasons that the best way to live is to '... stave off regret. That's what the whole thing's about. And we can't stave it off for ever, because it is impossible not to make the mistakes that let regret in, but the best of us manage to limp on into our sixties or seventies before we succumb,' (p. 201).

Key Issue: Guilt

Nick Hornby's main characters don't want to feel guilty any more. Their attempts to be good disappoint them because they do not manage to escape their guilty feelings. Katie feels guilty about nearly everything, from committing adultery to homelessness to not being able to solve all her patients' problems. So in this final study, we look at guilt. Why do we feel guilty anyway? What does the Bible say about our attempts to make amends for hurting people? Should we feel guilty? What does the Bible's promise of a new start really mean?

Bible Study

Choose one question from each section.

1. Guilty conscience

Who wants to be someone like me? People like us? Because we're almost always sure that we're wrong; we're almost always sure that we will go to hell, even though an inordinate amount of our waking thoughts are directed towards achieving the opposite effect. We know what's right but we don't do it because it's too hard, it asks too much ... (Katie, p. 125)

- Read Romans 2:12–16 and 25–29. Were the Gentiles off the hook because they did not have God's law? Were the Jews off the hook because they had been circumcised? How does the conscience work?

  Leaders: At this point in Romans, Paul is establishing that being born a Jew doesn't count for anything before God in and of itself. What matters is the heart.

- Read Titus 1:5–16. How were those with corrupted consciences leading others astray? In what ways were the elders to help Christians to be pure?

  Leaders: Paul is concerned at the damaging influence of false teachers — especially those that he calls the 'circumcision group'. These people apparently were insisting that Gentile Christians should follow the Jewish law and, in particular, be circumcised.

2. Making amends

'Reversal. That's what we're calling it. You take something you've done wrong, or some bad you've done to someone, and you reverse it. Do the opposite. If you stole something you give it back. If you were horrible, you have to be nice.' (GoodNews, p. 176)

- Read 1 Samuel 25:1–35. How would you describe Abigail's response to the situation? What did her actions achieve for Nabal and David?

- Read Matthew 5:21–26. Why does Jesus say we must make amends before approaching God? How does it make a difference to us?

3. Conviction

I don't wish to be melodramatic: I know I have not lived a bad life. But nor do I think that this crime-sheet amounts to nothing: believe me, it amounts to something. Look at it. Adultery. The casual exploitation of friends. Disrespect for parents who have done nothing apart from attempt to stay close to me. I mean, that's two of the ten commandments broken already, and given that — what, three, four? — of the ten are all about Sunday working hours and graven images, stuff that no longer really applies in early twenty-first-century Holloway, I'm looking at a thirty-three per cent strike rate, and that, to me, is too high. (Katie, p. 180)

- Read Ezra 9:1–10:4. Why was Ezra so appalled at the Israelites' guilt? What effect did his prayer have?

- Read 2 Corinthians 7:8–13a. How were the Corinthians convicted of their sin? What is the difference between godly sorrow and worldly sorrow?

4. Starting again — 'a clean sheet'

When I look at my sins (and if I think they're sins, then they are sins), I can see the appeal of born-again Christianity. I suspect that it's not the Christianity that is so alluring; it's the rebirth. Because who wouldn't wish to start all over again? (Katie, p. 181)

- Read Titus 2:11–3:8. How does God give us a fresh start? What difference does this make to how we live our lives?

- Read Hebrews 10:1–25. What has Jesus done to deal with our guilt? Having being put right with God, how does the writer encourage us to live?

Implications

I get up in the morning determined to do something approximating to the right thing, and within two hours find something else to feel guilty about. (Katie, p. 185)

Choose one or more of the following questions.

- Some psychologists distinguish between real guilt and false guilt. Do you identify with that distinction and how do you deal with each?
- Take time to examine your conscience, asking God to speak to you through it.
- How can you make amends for the ways in which you have hurt others?
- What would you say to someone who says they still feel guilty about something, no matter how many times they repent about it?
- How would you talk to Katie about the real possibility of a new start?
- How much are you living in the freedom of God's grace? What does it mean to be circumcised in your heart, by the Spirit (Rom 2:29)?
- Do you put rules on yourself or others to justify yourself?

Prayer

Spend some time praying through these issues.

Background Reading

You will find links to some background reading on the Connect Bible Studies website: www.connectbiblestudies.com/uk/catalogue/0007/background.htm

Discuss

Discuss this study in the online discussion forums at www.connectbiblestudies.com/discuss

Members' Sheet: How to be Good — Part 4

Summary

As a GP, Katie has always found plenty to feel guilty about — she constantly has to deal with patients who are let down through lack of resources and drugs that never work. Recently, though, her guilty conscience has thrived on personal troubles that she certainly has more control over. Problems with her husband, David, have affected the whole family. Katie feels particularly guilty now that she has secretly moved out of the family home to live in a bedsit: 'I have woken most nights since then at 2.25 am precisely, feeling bereft and lonely and guilty and frantic with worry and fear, and it takes me ages to get back to sleep. And yet I wake up in the morning feeling fresh,' (p. 172). Herein lies the source of her anxiety — she feels that it is her duty to be at home but she wants and needs the space to get her life back together.

Katie recognises the deep-rooted need to be forgiven and start over again, but cannot see a realistic way that this can be achieved. Instead, she reasons that the best way to live is to '... stave off regret. That's what the whole thing's about. And we can't stave it off for ever, because it is impossible not to make the mistakes that let regret in, but the best of us manage to limp on into our sixties or seventies before we succumb,' (p. 201).

Key Issue

Bible Study notes

Implications

Prayer